THE YALE DRAMA SERIES

David Charles Horn Foundation

The Yale Drama Series is funded by the generous support of the David Charles Horn Foundation, established in 2003 by Francine Horn to honor the memory of her husband, David. In keeping with David Horn's lifetime commitment to the written word, the David Charles Horn Foundation commemorates his aspirations and achievements by supporting new initiatives in the literary and dramatic arts.

Bottle Fly

JACQUELINE GOLDFINGER

Foreword by Nicholas Wright

Yale UNIVERSITY PRESS   NEW HAVEN & LONDON

Yale University Press books may be purchased in quantity for educational, business, or promotional use. For information, please e-mail sales.press@yale.edu (U.S. office) or sales@yaleup.co.uk (U.K. office).

Set in Galliard type by Integrated Publishing Solutions, Grand Rapids, Michigan.

Printed in the United States of America.

ISBN 978-0-300-23501-2 (hardcover : alk. paper)

Library of Congress Control Number: 2018935050

A catalogue record for this book is available from the British Library.

This paper meets the requirements of ANSI/NISO Z39.48-1992 (Permanence of Paper).

10 9 8 7 6 5 4 3 2 1

For all enquiries regarding performance rights or rights in any kind of media, please contact Abrams Artists Agency, 275 Seventh Avenue, 26th Floor, New York, N.Y. 10001, Attn: Amy Wagner.

"What is your aim in Philosophy? To show the fly the way out of the fly-bottle."
—Ludwig Wittgenstein

Contents

Foreword

There are plenty of plays about falling in and out of love and many more about flirtation, frustration, desertion, and sexual madness. All of these are action-filled events, replete with change and transformation, so they transfer to the stage with brio.

But plays about love . . . unqualified love . . . are rare, surprisingly so when you consider how large a part it plays in our lives, or how deeply we want it to.

Bottle Fly, a play very much about love, was the winner of the Yale Drama Series award for 2017, when I judged the competition for my third and final year. This series receives about sixteen hundred entries annually from around the world: far more than any one person could read in a short space of time, so, as in previous years, I assembled a panel of friends and colleagues to help with the assessment: playwrights Howard Brenton, Rebecca Lenkiewicz, and Barney Norris; directors Jeff James, Indhu Rubasingham, Amelia Sears, and Matthew Xia; National Theatre dramaturg Tom Lyons; former Channel Four commissioning editor Peter Ansorge, and the Faber editorial director for drama, Dinah Wood.

I followed the system that my predecessor, David Hare,

had introduced. The plays were divided up among the panel members to read. We then assembled for our first meeting around my large kitchen table, food provided and wine moderately consumed. We drew on what we'd read to propose our candidates for the top slot: we described the plays and we sold them to the others as convincingly as we could. Questions, interrogation, and friendly argument brought the short list down to as many candidates for the prize as there were people doing the judging: eleven in this case.

Our second meeting was held once we had all read the plays on the short list. The important discussion took place next: it was friendly, frank, and revelatory not only about the plays but about each other. There were many things that we all shared, not least a love of drama and a lot of experience in it. But we were widely different in age, although, interestingly, there appeared to be no correlation between age and any particular set of views.

I found this exchange between the generations to be a complete joy. It occurred to me, as I looked around the table, that there were people there for whom Howard Brenton was a legendary figure, whose work and influence they might have studied as students. Yet no judge of any age could have been a more zestful advocate for what was new and original. I admired the cool analyses of Peter Ansorge, remembering as I did his historic contribution to a great age of British television drama. Of the older people in the room, the oldest was probably me: twelve months later, I still quote to myself the keen perceptions of panel members several generations younger than I am. It's less common than it ought to be for a variety of theater people to get together around a table and talk in a serious way about our art. We should do it more often. Better decisions would be made that way, I think, and better plays produced.

Unlike some competitions, the Yale Drama Series doesn't require an entrant to be supported by a literary manager or an agent: anyone can send their play to be considered. The other good thing about it—and I recommend this for all literary competitions—is that plays are considered blind: the judging panel has no idea of the playwright's name, age, address, gender, or cultural heritage.

This led to an odd moment at one of our later meetings, when I asked whether any of us had speculated about the author of a particular play. Was the writer a he, a she, or a neither? Was the playwright white or a person of colour? The answer, it turned out, was that nobody had thought about it. I hadn't either and I felt slightly sticky even to have asked. It's striking how completely issues of race and gender fall away when they aren't forced on you.

What did I notice most about the plays we read? More than anything else, how bold they were. The range of imagination and invention was sometimes dizzying. Play after play took me to a place I'd never expected and never been to, geographically, psychologically, or socially. The world of nightmare was a common locale. So was the future, awkward, menacing, and dystopian. The dead came alive and monsters paced the streets. Poverty was a recurrent theme, and so were the perilous expedients by which the poor tried to escape it. Suburbia was corrupt and louche. Family life came up less often than in previous years and, when it did, it was destructive and bizarre.

Skimming the notes I made at the time, I notice the darkness of the tone that they reflect: how often our plays portrayed the world as a dangerous place from which escape into a secret, personal realm is also dangerous. Was this a reflection of the world we live in? Did these plays hand back to us, in an enhanced, more readable form, the real-life world in which we live, a place of violence, lies, deceptions, and occasional joys? Of course: that is what plays do.

Bottle Fly is an ambitious work. Most plays are written in a kind of slimmed-down epic form: they show events and states and people changing over a lateral stretch of time. But this play's subject—love—has a marked imperviousness to time and the extent to which it changes is a complex question. Shakespeare claimed that love never changes at all—"it is an ever-fixéd mark,"—which, if true, would make love dramatically impossible. The truth is probably more subtle than he suggests: true love, deep love, changes so slowly and so incrementally that often neither lover notices what's going on until the transformation is complete: hence the shock when one lover takes an unexpected look at the other and sees a stranger.

The direction of such a play, then, is not lateral but vertical: it dives into the hidden depths of a common emotion that we all have felt, and suffered from, and been grateful for. *Bottle Fly* illuminates love in many guises: love for those who have mattered to one in the past, love that was born as pity, love tinged with guilt, love for those who need your protection, and love for someone who, without even knowing that she was doing it, holds out the promise of a more beautiful life.

It's that last variety of love that stopped me in my tracks in my first reading. A middle-aged academic remembers the moment at a filling station where love struck like a bolt of lightning out of a clear sky and changed her life forever. The off-stage scene that she describes could not have been more vivid to me if the entire filling station had been transported on to the stage, complete with pumps and a line of cars. I'll never forget it.

As ever, I liked and admired a number of plays that, for one reason or another, were crowded out in the final lap by other competitors. I hope they will have a further life. In recognition that a single winner can tell only part of the story, we chose two excellent, promising plays as runners-up: *Cottontail*, by Andrew Rosendorf, and *Natives*, by Carla Grauls.

But the winner was *Bottle Fly*, by the fine American playwright Jacqueline Goldfinger.

Here it is.

Nicholas Wright

Bottle Fly

Special Thanks: Francine Horn, Playwright Nicholas Wright, Dramaturg Alix Rosenfeld, the PlayPenn New Play Conference, the Yale Drama Prize, and The National Theatre in London

Time/Place: Present day. An old barn reconstituted into a bar near the Everglades in rural Florida.

People: 4 Females, 1 Male

K   20s, Woman, open ethnicity, otherworldly in a hard-packed red-clay way; cannot speak, sings instead

ROSIE   40s, White woman, owns and runs the bar; Cal's wife

CAL   40s, Man of color, Rosie's husband; oil rig worker

RUTH   50, Woman, open ethnicity, looking for answers later in life; Penny's lover

PENNY   20s, Woman, open ethnicity but first preference is Seminole or Hispanic; tough, bee keeper–tradition keeper

Florida is an incredibly ethnically diverse state and the Everglades region is reflective of that diversity.

Accent
Florida is a bizarre state with many variations on the Southern accent. Do not worry about the accent. Just go with the rhythm and flow of the words. These folks talk as they live: hard, fast, with heat.

Music
This is a play with music. You can license short-term, acappella live performance rights. Licensing information is available at the back of the script. If you do not want to license the music, a list of replacement songs in the public domain that are less recognizable but work well within the play is available from the playwright.

Elements of Style
A slash (/word/) indicates overlapping speech.
Brackets [word] indicate an unspoken word. A sound and/or movement should express the word's meaning.
Dots after a character's name . . . means that something unspoken yet meaningful is going on between the characters.

Act One
1. Early That Morning

As lights rise, we see an old ramshackle barn. The barn is two stories high and wide enough to store twelve-foot stalks of sugar cane. The walls can be wood planks or aluminum sheets. Regardless, there are holes in the walls after decades of use. Paper and newsprint have been pasted over the holes.

The first floor of the barn has been repurposed. It is now a small rural bar with a few mismatched tables and chairs. There's an old army cot in the corner. There are three exits: one to an off-stage first-floor bedroom, one to the porch leading outside, and a ladder leading up to a small loft.

The second floor is the small loft. We cannot see into the loft but can see the ladder used for entrance and exit.

K (female, 20s, earthy, a little slow) sits on the army cot on the first floor.

K sings beautifully; flawed and raw but with an underlying grace.

K *(sings* Dream a Little Dream of Me*)*   Stars shining bright above you,
Night breezes whisper I love you,
Bees buzzing in the sycamore tree,
Dream a little dream of me.

From the second-floor loft, we begin to hear the low buzzing of bees.

K *(sings)*   Say "night-ie-night" and kiss me.
Just hold me tight and . . .
(tries to push across the chasm between her mouth and her brain)
. . .
And . . .
And . . . you can,
Dream a little dream of me.

The buzzing from the loft gets louder.

K *sings louder to push them away.*

K *(sings)*   SWEET DREAMS TILL SUN-BEAMS FIND YOU,
Sweet dreams that leave all worries behind you,
But in your dreams whatever they be,
Whatever they be.
Whatever they beee.

The buzzing is monstrously loud. The bees are flying down from the loft and descending upon K.

K *tries to get away.*

K *(sings)*   Beee. Beeeee. Beeeeeeeeee.
DREAM A LITTLE DREAM OF—

K *screams, slaps at the bees.*

K   BeeeeeeeBeeeeeeeeeeeeeeeeeeeeeeeeeeeeeeeeeDreeeee-
aaaaammmmmmmm . . . gggg.aghhhh . . . Dreeeeeeem
. . .

ROSIE *(female, 40s, white, tough) enters, wears a bathrobe and holds a fly swatter. She swats the bees away from* K *like a momma bear.*

ROSIE   /Goddamned motherfuckers/

K   /aaaaaalittttttttllllllllleeee . . . ggggg.achhhhh . . . ghhhhh . . . /

ROSIE *(calls to the loft)*   /Jesus H!/

K   /eammmmmmmmm. . . . offffffffmeeeeeeeeee . . . /

ROSIE   /*Fucking!*/

K   /ahhhhguuhhhhguhhhhh/

ROSIE   /Christ!/

K   /Meeeeeeeeeeeeee./

The buzzing retreats. The bees fly back up to the loft.

ROSIE *comforts* K.

ROSIE   It's okay. Hey, girl, K, girl,

K   Ackhggggghhh

ROSIE   Shhhh, just, shhhhh now,
Where is it? Where is it?

ROSIE *feels around in* K*'s pockets.*

K *(sings in fear and pain)*   Dreamalittledreamofmedream alittledreamofmedreamalittledreamofmedreamalittledream ofme.

ROSIE   It's gonna be,
Okay.
It's gonna be,
I'm gonna evict those snatch-eating bitches.
You'll see, you'll see, okay, okay, here girl.

ROSIE *pulls an antique crystal doorknob out of* K*'s pocket.*
Gives it to her.

ROSIE   Here.

K *accepts it like communion. She rubs it. She calms down.*

K *(sings)*   DDDDDDD . . .
Dream a little dream of me.

ROSIE   I know, honey, I know.
It's o—
It's gonna be, okay.
I got you.
I got you.

K   . . .

ROSIE   It's gonna be okay.
Miss Rosie got you.
You're my dream girl,
My perfect dream.

K   [Yes, I am. I am.]
. . .
[And I am safe.]
. . .

RUTH*'s voice is heard from the off-stage loft.*

RUTH'S VOICE *(from loft, off-stage)*   I am so, so sorry
about that.

ROSIE *screams up to* RUTH.

ROSIE   Pack your bags!
And your damn bees!
And get out!

RUTH'S VOICE *(from loft, off-stage)*   It will not happen
again. I swear—

ROSIE   K got, she got,
Stings.
She's got damn, what look like she walk through nettles,
Spanish bayonets, palm stickers, and shit.
All up on her arms.
All over her,
Good thing she dressed.
Otherwise, she'd be all eaten up, even in her private places.
You got to take them and go.

RUTH *(50, female, uncomfortable in her own skin) appears
at the top of the loft ladder.*

RUTH   /I was just checking/

ROSIE   /Like I fucking care/

RUTH   /As it got colder.
Just checking/

ROSIE   /Do you not hear me, girl?/

RUTH   /Making sure the bees feed./

ROSIE   /You deaf, dumb, and—/

RUTH   /Please let me—/

RUTH *descends the ladder awkwardly. She is not used to this.*

As RUTH *descends,* PENNY *(20s, female, muscled, farm-hand healthy) enters from outside, wears work gloves, pants, boots, and lugs an empty beehive.*

ROSIE *does not see* PENNY *enter.*

ROSIE *(to* RUTH*)*   /You deaf, dumb, and a pussy licker?
That's three strikes,
An' you out, bitch.

PENNY   Hey!

ROSIE *sees* PENNY.

RUTH *(to* PENNY*)*   It's okay, hon.

PENNY *ignores* RUTH *and addresses* ROSIE.

PENNY *(to* ROSIE*)*   We paid through the month.
And we fixed the roof—

ROSIE *(lies)*   Not much fixin' to be done.

PENNY   The big hole.
In the south corner.
Ripped off in that last blow.
You gonna tell me?

ROSIE   Listen, I didn't ask for—

PENNY   You didn't not ask for—

ROSIE   Nobody asked for K to get all bit up by your
damn bees neither.

That shuts PENNY *up.*

PENNY   That's truth.

PENNY *goes up the ladder, tosses the hive into the loft. Hangs
on the ladder. Takes off her work gloves and boots, tosses them
up after the hive.*

RUTH   I am really so sorry about that.
I would never—

ROSIE   Well you did.

RUTH   —Intentionally—

ROSIE   Road to hell—

RUTH   It was an accident.
It won't happen again.

ROSIE   —Paved smooth with 'em.

RUTH   Just an accide—

ROSIE   K got a place here.
No questions asked. K got one.
K can do what she wants.
But you just money guests.
You know what money guests is?

PENNY   We kno—

ROSIE   Not you,
She.
(to RUTH*)*
You know what money guests is, Ruth?

RUTH   I, I, I, I don't but
I get the sense, the feeling that your,
Connotation is that—

PENNY *descends the ladder.*

ROSIE   Money guests means I got to house you.
Got to feed you. Because I need your money.
But you not a real guest.
You don't got no real place here.
K,
She's, got a
Real place here.

PENNY   Yeah, but we pay all the same,
So we some kind of guests.
The kinda ones you need.
(re: RUTH*)*
So back offa' her.
And we gonna be big-money guests soon.
So you best be nice, or we'll take our big-money guest
selves off somewhere else.

RUTH *goes to* K.

RUTH   I'm so sorry, K.

K *(confusion)* . . .

RUTH   Okay?
It won't happen ever again.
The bees, I won't drop their hive, ever again.

K *(forgiveness)*   . . .
(release)
. . .

K *puts the crystal doorknob back into her pocket.*

RUTH   Okay.
See, we're all fine.

ROSIE . . .

PENNY . . .

RUTH . . .

ROSIE . . .

PENNY . . .

RUTH . . .

ROSIE . . .   Shit. Fine.
. . .
But you only paid through the rest of the month.
Then I want this shit out of here. You and your beasts.

RUTH   She can't harvest until the summer.

PENNY *(quietly to* RUTH*)*   Let it lie.

RUTH   But Rosie needs to understand—

PENNY   Let me do it!
Just, sorry, just
Let me do it. My way.
Please.

ROSIE *(to* PENNY*)*   You think you a man now, girl, you
think, you a husband or somethin'?
Get on out right now, you thinkin' that, goin' 'gainst God,
Nature, an' Good Sense.

RUTH *(to* ROSIE*)*   Look, lesbians have been around since,
The Isle of Lesbos, in Ancient Greece, was—

ROSIE   I'm gonna throw up.

PENNY *silences* RUTH *with a hand on her arm. Moves her
toward the ladder.*

PENNY   Nothin' much you can get out of anger.
Let her cool.
(to ROSIE*)*
Dawn cracked.
Might as well get up and out for the day.

PENNY *and* RUTH *climb up the ladder to the loft.*

ROSIE   Might as well.

ROSIE *checks on* K.

ROSIE   You okay, Lady K?

K *nods.*

ROSIE *folds* K*'s blanket.*

PENNY *disappears into the loft.*

RUTH*'s at the top of the ladder.*

RUTH   So sorry, again.
I'm really, I'm just clumsy, I guess.

ROSIE   [That] Don't make up for it.
Think 'bout where you're gonna go to at the end of the
month.
Sure as shit ain't gonna be here.

RUTH *disappears into the loft.*

K   [I got to go soon, too.]
. . .
. . .

ROSIE   No, you ain't got to go nowhere, lady bug.
Not ever, ever.
Don't you worry about that.

K   [I got to.]
. . .
. . .

ROSIE   They'll clear out.
It'll just be us again.
And Daddy Cal.
Cal'll be home soon, we'll have a little party.
Just the three of us, once they're gone.
Just us, love.

K   [I'm sorry.]
. . .
IIIII . . . ghhgh . . .
. . .
Ssssssss. . . .

ROSIE   Shhhhhhh . . .
No, no, no. Don't you worry. Here.
(puts her hand on the door knob in K's pocket)
Hold on to that and let me get my day things on.

K *(sings* In the Still of the Night*)* . . . ghhhh . . .
Innnn. . . .
IIIIIIn the still of the night

ROSIE   Oh, I like this one.

K *(sings)*   As I gaze from my window,
At the moon in its flight,
My thoughts all stray to you.

In the still of the night
While the world is in slumber,
Oh, the times without number,
Darling when I say to you

ROSIE   I love you, my girl.
[I'll] Be right back.

K *(sings)*   "Do you love me, as I do you?
Are you my life to be, My dream come true?"

ROSIE *exits.*

K *(sings)*   "Or will this dream of mine fade out of sight.
Like the moon, growing dim,
On the rim of the hill,
In the chill,
Still,
Of the night?"

*Warm light streams through the paper that covers the walls of
the barn; the transcendent connection between* K*'s seen and
unseen worlds. (For a visual reference, see John Fraser's
"Collage Works* 1994–2002.*")*

Later, when K *speaks to the audience, warm light shines
through the paper, bathing her world in a transcendent glow,*

*a visible connection of the seen and unseen worlds, a past and
future perfect that contain her reality.*

K *stands tall and straight for the first time, her inner self
freed from the constraints of her outer shell.*

*She takes the crystal doorknob out of her pocket, tosses it in the
air, catches it, puts it back.*

She addresses the audience.

K   She touched my fault-line and I awoke.
The first time, on the side of a knotted dirt road, run red
with streaks of clay and white with streaks of sand, lapping
up my unknowingness, she woke me.
I had slept in that field since . . . like discarded lumber.
Since . . . being laid fallow, by the death of love.
Since being made gone, by a family, government issued at
birth, that never transformed water into wine, paperwork
into blood.
. . .
It was too much.
. . .
I don't blame them.
They finally had their own baby, didn't need a pretend
one, and grandma had been left to the ground. So they set
me free. To be found.
(looks to ROSIE*'s room)*
She stroked my forehead.
She brought down the fever.
She fed me.
She gave me a blanket.
She called me K.
And when I came back around,
I woke to a life inside my life.
To this, screaming echo layered like paper on paper,
decade on decade.

The doctor says the talking part of the brain is different
from the singing part.
He says, it's a blessing from God that she can do anything
really,
After that delivery. No air. She could be full stupid, not
just half.

I learned the songs my government-issued grandmother
had played on the record player across long humid
afternoons.
Her sounds squeezing through walls of water thicker than
school paste a heavy drip drop drip drop drop drop drop
down into my ears.
I spent hours there, listening, afraid moving would break
the sound, afraid to sweat, to stink, to make myself dirty
and unacceptable within the beautiful noise.
The music pushed away the stink and rot of my days.
Pushed away the unlucky in life and love.
The music my companion.
My drunk translator.
(looks to ROSIE*'s room)*
The bees know, that I don't make her happy any more.
That she's sick of me, like my first family got, after grand-
mother's death.
The bees, they sing themselves so they understand.
They hear.
They know.
And they punished me.
I should go,
So Cal will stay home,
So life will be easier,
So she will be happy.
I can't tell her: I love you. I am grateful for you. I know
I make everything wrong, and that's why the bees, they
weren't stinging me. They were just singing me away.
I can't say,

Not in a way that she will understand.
Goodbye.
(sings)
Like the moon, growing dim,
On the rim of the hill,
In the chill,
Still,
Of the night.
K *returns to her slumped form.*

Lights return to normal.

There's a soft humming of bees from the loft, and some almost imperceptible laughing and chatting.

ROSIE *enters in day clothes, carries a bag of peanuts, a cookie sheet, and a small bucket.*

She sits across from K.

They shell peanuts. The nuts go onto a cookie sheet for toasting, the shells go into a bucket to be thrown out.

The nuts make a soft rhythmic "plink" when they hit the cookie sheet.

Plink. Plink. Plink. Plink. Plink. Plink.

There's a thump from the loft. And then another. A stifled "Oops!"

ROSIE *throws the nuts harder onto the sheet.*

Plink Plink PlinkPlinkPlinkPlinkPlink.

Another thump and a loud shushing.

ROSIE *throws 'em harder and faster.*

PLINKPLINKPLINKPLINKPLINK PLINKPLINK-
PLINKPLINKPLINK PLINKPLINKPLINK-
PLINKPLINK
The thumps and shushes and occasional muffled laughter
continue until ROSIE *is throwing the nuts so hard onto the*
cookie sheet that they sound like hail on a tin roof.

The nuts bounce off the cookie sheet and onto the floor. K *bends*
down to pick them up, but the falling nuts hit her on the
head. They hurt!

PLINKPLINKPLINKPLINKPLINK PLINKPLINK-
PLINKPLINKPLINK PLINKPLINKPLINK-
PLINKPLINK
There's a continuous series of bangs and a loud moan and
that's finally too much for ROSIE:

ROSIE   Swear to God,
You don't get those hands outta those cooters and get
down here for lunch, I'm gonna snatch 'em out myself.

The banging and moaning stop.

RUTH *(off-stage from loft)*   Well, that would be quite
rude.

PENNY *(from off-stage loft) (to* RUTH*)*   Shhhh.
(calls down stairs)
Sorry, Sorry Miss Rosie.
We didn't think you could hear.

ROSIE *(to* K*)*   You just wait.
When Cal gets home,
When he gets back, they'll stop.

They will.
Can't be doin' all that in front of a man.

K   [Um, they probably will keep on?]

PENNY *comes down the ladder with a small glass jar of honey
still on the comb.*

PENNY   Thought you could use this for the peanut
butter.
Drop it into the blender, instead of the oil,
Make it cream and smooth,
And Sweet.
Orange Blossom Honey sweet.
For Cal.
(telling)
I hear he likes your peanut butter and honey.

ROSIE *(blushes, 'cause he does)*   Don't be gross.
Good Lord.

K *laughs.*

ROSIE *(good natured) (to* K*)*   Enough outta you.
(to PENNY*)*
End of the month.

PENNY   Come now.

RUTH *comes down the ladder.*

RUTH   Sorry. Again. So sorry.
Didn't mean to—

ROSIE   What cha'll mean don't matter.
What you do matters.

RUTH   So I just can't do anything right?

ROSIE   No, not particularly.
How 'bout y'all do something useful for once?
Just sittin' up there, watchin' those bees do their business,
How about you do some business?
How about you find something useful to do?
Ain't gonna find no lazy-ass reparations bullshit around
here.
Money don't fall off trees.
Waitin' for bees to do a job for you, so you can reap what
they sow,
What kinda business is that?

RUTH   It's the kind that will save the world.
Re-pollination.
Colony collapse is a significant concern in the broader
environmental spectrum of—

ROSIE   Shut the fuck up.
Bees right here. We right here. It's fine.
All I want to know is what you gonna do? For yourself.
For my girl you got stung up so bad.
How you gonna say sorry?

PENNY *(to* K*)*   Hey K.
Hey girl.
How about we go out on a boat today?
You like that?

K   [You're talking to me?]
. . .

PENNY   Yeah, you wanna go.
Out, on the water, feel the wind in your hair,
Cool water spray up your arms,
On your face.

K   [Heck, yeah]

. . .

ROSIE   You ain't takin' her out on no boat.
You don't got no boat to take her out in.

PENNY   I got a friend who's got one.
We'll make it a great day for K.
(to K*)*
We'll ride down some side stream
Ain't no one else seen before.
Undisturbed, the way it first was laid out,
Like God's own image over the dark earth.
They say He spread out his hand, stretched his fingers
wide,
Pressed his palm hard down into the mud,
An' that dent in all his creation is the Everglades.
It's the only piece of this earth that's shaped just like him,
Like his outstretched hand,
And so He filled it with all the best things.
Alligators, turtles, great blue herons, egrets, maybe even a
panther or two.

K *is excited.*

ROSIE   You can really take her on a boat ride?

PENNY   I can.
I know a guy.
I've been drivin' since I was knee high to a honey bee.
Let us go?
Let us be use-ful, for a day.
Let us make amends.

ROSIE   . . .

. . .

. . .

K   [Please!]

. . .

. . .

ROSIE   Okay.

But be careful.

An' take her raincoat, for the wind and water.

It's out dryin' on the porch.

An' make sure her hair stays tied back so that the salt don't get too far down into it. Salt on the scalp'll make her itch for weeks. And—

K *kisses* ROSIE *on the cheek.*

ROSIE   Okay.

Stay safe.

And listen to 'em. You hear me, K?

You listen good.

K *nods.*

Lights shift.

2. That Night

PENNY and CAL *(40s, male, full of regret) sit at the bar drinking beer.*

PENNY   Daddy and Momma always pretended it wasn't real.
Like it was just girls being friends.

CAL   Instead a' girlfriends.

PENNY   Yeah.
But then they walked in on me with the neighbor girl.

CAL   Can't come back from that.

PENNY   Nope.
Lickin' your girlfriend's asshole
In your parents' marriage bed
Pretty much says it all.

CAL *nods.*

They drink.

CAL   . . .
. . .

PENNY   . . .

CAL   I got a family to think about. And other folks threw y'all out.

PENNY *nods.*

CAL   Well, they know your daddy.
And your daddy's daddy.
And he ain't shy about advertising The Exile.

PENNY   Yeah, well, he can go fuck himself.

CAL *laughs.*

CAL   Yeah, you sure his.

PENNY   I ain't none of that man.
What he put up in people's faces,
Like he got,
Walkin' around like Jesus gave him grazing rights on the
fields of morality never plowed. Like he's fuckin',
Like he never—

CAL   Just like him.

PENNY *(a threat)*   Hey!
(more control)
I'm sayin',
It comes up on you like a a a a a a a a
A blade of light in the shade.
Like you under an old oak tree in the afternoon
Laid out underneath on a blanket,
Eyes closed, drowsing.
And all a sudden the breeze shifts,
The branches shading you move, just a millimeter and just
for a second,
And for one frightening and glorious moment
A little blade of light cuts right through your eyelid, a
burst of reds and oranges explode and you almost feel that
you can see something beyond sense. That you can see,
through, things to the heart of the matter. In blindness
there is the only real sight and for a split second you feel,
Glorious. Transcendent. Special. Right with the world.

CAL   I don't see what that's—

PENNY   Like out on the rig.
You got moments when everything feels, strong and right.

CAL   . . .

PENNY   Yeah, you do. I see it.
Daddy always wanted things to be right, be good,
But then when that right comes along,
That gift from,
I don't believe in God no more,
But that gift from the natural world that makes us, almost-
angels, helps you taste a bit of what's sweet, so you can live
this life a little easier,
He says "no." He says—

CAL   Get out my house.

PENNY   Yeah.
(looks up to loft)
But we got to stay, stay put until harvest season,
Because I got all the bees I raised,
By myself, my lot, since I was little.
I got 'em all up there, and I can't afford to move 'em,
To move us, to get,
I got to get my feet under me.
I need somewhere that blade of light
And my clay feet
Can live together in peace,
But that takes money and time.

CAL   And Rosie don't want to give you that.

PENNY   No shit.
. . .

(come on, you know)

. . .

. . .

CAL   I got this ex-Marine on the oil rig. White boy.
A ginzel, a rookie, on the rig at least.
He in the bunk right under me.
I come off a twenty-four-hour shift. Rough one.
Hurricane storm tipped us,
Ride like a roller coaster that keeps you drownin'.
You feel like, I'm gonna drown on a dry boat,
You feel like, you touch that forever in a quick moment.

. . .

You up in the rig, tryin' to keep it all together,
While you tossed around harder than bowling pins.
This substitute, boy, he says that he looked at me out
there,
On that riggin', keepin' the whole bit together with my
bare hands,
An' I come back in,
An' he laughs an' says, you looked like the devil out there.
That's how I always thought the devil looked.
A big dark strong thing, pullin' everythin' apart.

. . .

I was holdin' it together, I says.
I's holdin' the world together for twelve hours while you
slept.
An' he just laughed again and said,
"Sure Mr. Devil Man, sure. Don't get my bunk wet."
He walks off.
He thinks he's sleepin' right below the Devil hisself out in
a rig in the Gulf.
'Cause a' what he's been told to see,
Not what he actually seen.

. . .

I don't know if what you two get up to in that loft is . . .

I don't know.
But I know you ain't hateful.
You seein' what you is, not what you told.
I know you fixed Rosie's roof so the rain don't blow in
when I'm away.
I know that you'd protect K, when it comes to it,
That you jumped in alligator water for her today.
I don't think it'd hurt too much if y'all stay until the
harvest.

PENNY   Your wife don't see it that way.

CAL   I'll let her know my mind.
She takes that into account. Sometimes.

PENNY *laughs.*

CAL   Don't laugh now.
(re: telling ROSIE*)*
Just got to find the right time.

PENNY *stops laughing.*

They drink.

PENNY   . . .
. . .

CAL   . . .
. . .

K, RUTH, *and* ROSIE *enter.*

K *has a bandage around her foot, limps.*

CAL *goes to* K. *Helps her sits down, kisses her on the top of the head.*

ROSIE *is pissed off.*

CAL *(to* ROSIE*)*   Hello, my love.

ROSIE   I hope you put that beer on her tab.

CAL   She jumped in after—

ROSIE   Oh, after,
Well, after does a whole lot of good,
When you fall in the water before.
I mean it's that deep—

CAL *kisses her, which shuts her up, for a minute.*

ROSIE   —after the rains an' all and—

CAL *kisses her again.*

ROSIE   —it's not like she can swim.

CAL *kisses.*

ROSIE   I mean, it's not that deep,
But it's slippery.

CAL *(to* PENNY*)*   Y'all just gonna have to let her finish.

ROSIE *(to* CAL*)*   This is not funny, Cal.
(to PENNY*)*
You shoulda called sooner. Right when it happened.
I coulda been there sooner.

PENNY *(pulls a phone out of her pocket)*   No service out
there.

ROSIE   Well, she's in pain most the afternoon 'cause a'
you.

CAL *(to* ROSIE*)*   Come on, Rosie. I missed you.

RUTH *settles* K *at her table.*

ROSIE *goes to* CAL.

ROSIE, CAL *and* PENNY *settle at the bar.*

ROSIE   And that man at the hospital—

PENNY   The doctor?

ROSIE   No, the other one.

RUTH   The orderly.

ROSIE   NO! That man who carries—

PENNY/CAL   The orderly.

ROSIE   Well, you don't have to gang up on me.
So this other man, this orderly,
He comes up to us,
Like we're trash in the bucket,
He comes up and he says, she can walk to her room.
And I says, no sir, no she cannot walk. Look at her foot.
He says, she's a strong one. She's a buck. She be fine.
You swamp people, you can take it.
And he wheels away.
Motherfucker pushes the wheelchair the other direction.
So I go on up to him . . .

RUTH   She did. She really did.

ROSIE   . . . I go on up and I stand right in front of that
chair,
And I stop him,
And I says, what that mean, what you say, what that mean
exactly?
And he looks at me all like . . .

ROSIE *makes a condescending face.*

RUTH   He did. He then—

ROSIE   I say, you mean it's okay she be in pain,
She hurts, because, why, because we don't live in town.
We live hard and you gotta make it harder?
Then he gets this flush all over him.
And he says, it was a compliment.
And I says, ain't no compliment, if my girl hurting,
You take care of her.
You supposed to ease suffering, motherfucker,
Not keep it on. Not some folks meant to suffer
More than others
On your say so.
'Cause they walk across fields to work.
There's no glory in suffering that can be eased.
So you gonna wheel your skinny ass around right now
And you gonna pick up my girl
And you gonna roll her over to her room as gentle as a
mother hen warming a newborn chick. Otherwise, you
gonna see who's gonna suffer today.
. . .
. . .

CAL   And?

ROSIE   I never did see a black boy go white as a bed
sheet.
K got her ride to her room.

RUTH   In silence.

PENNY   She's fixed now though.

ROSIE   She be okay.
(to K*)*
Right, K, baby? You be okay?

K *nods.*

ROSIE   Good girl.

CAL   Well, I'm glad of that.

RUTH   We all are.

ROSIE *(to* RUTH*)*   You just out to annoy me today.

RUTH   What now?

ROSIE *(to* CAL*)*   I tol' them, they got to leave.
They stung up K.
Battered her foot to pieces.

PENNY   We got her right out.
She leaned over to look for fish and—

ROSIE   And got a sprained ankle.

PENNY   Yeah, well . . . happens.

ROSIE *(disdain)*   Happens.

ROSIE *pops open a beer for* CAL*, hands it to him.*

PENNY *signals "My beer's done, too."*

PENNY . . .
. . .

ROSIE . . .
. . .

PENNY . . .

ROSIE *relents, pops one for her.*

ROSIE   This one's goin' on the tab.
(to CAL*)*
How long you got 'fore you go back?

CAL   Two days.

ROSIE   Two!

CAL   Two before my next hitch.
They got a new rig startin' up.
An intelligent well. With little robots that'll look after it,
After we set it up. Get it in running order.
Get it ready for electronic Toolhands to come in.
They'll be monitoring the wells from all the way up in
New York,
Out in California. Where ever those electric eyes go.

ROSIE   Itn't that what they pay management for?

CAL   No, they pay management to tell me
To get everythin' up and in runnin' order.

PENNY   That's some bullshit right there.

ROSIE   Yeah, it is.

PENNY *(overdoes it)*   Been gone eight weeks on an oil rig,
Only get two days off.
That's some ridiculousness right there.
That's some spiteful, hurtful, unnecessary,
I mean, it is. It is just—

ROSIE   I ain't gonna let you stay just 'cause
You agree
With me about it.

PENNY *shrugs. Didn't hurt to try.*

RUTH   I'm sure she didn't mean it like th—

PENNY *and* ROSIE *look to* RUTH:

RUTH   Oh, never mind.

ROSIE *(to* PENNY*)*   You need to shut that girl up.
Ever'time she opens her mouth—

ROSIE/PENNY   Flies come out.

ROSIE *(slowly, like* RUTH*'s stupid)*   That—means—that—
nothin'—good—comes—out.
Okay.
Get it, girl.

RUTH   Hey! I have a Ph.D.!

PENNY   Just ignore her, sweet—

ROSIE   What good's a P.H.—

RUTH   That means that I have been through many years
of education. I have written papers and a Master's disserta-
tion. I have defended a doctoral thesis.

PENNY   Hon, it's okay. Just ignore—

RUTH   I have sat on panels and reviewed grant applica-
tions and been awarded scholarships and residencies and
fellowships. I have citations. On paper. With with with
with gold seals. I have a bio longer than my arm, longer
than your arm, longer than both our arms. I have awards.
Awards given by people that matter to people that matter.
I have publications. And I lecture and and and and and I
know things! I do. I am a biochemical all-star. And you!
You can't treat me like—

ROSIE   That don't mean you're better than me.

RUTH   Maybe it does!
Maybe!
It . . . just . . . does.

CAL *moves away from* RUTH. *He thinks, "Oh, shit, girl. You
know not what you do."*

K *moves to get the crystal doorknob out of her pocket but her
hand comes up empty.*

PENNY   . . .
. . .

ROSIE   . . .
. . .

CAL   . . .
. . .

K *(looks at barren hands in sorrow)*   . . .
. . .

RUTH   . . .

. . .

ROSIE   . . .

. . .

RUTH   That's not what I meant.
I just mean, I mean . . .

ROSIE   I know what you mean.

RUTH   I just,
Everything I do here is wrong.
But everything I did out there was right.

ROSIE   Then why are you here?

RUTH *holds out her hand to* PENNY.

PENNY *takes it.*

RUTH   Because, she could see me.
I am seen.
In my old life, I was, they could,
Touch, the outside,
They could, acknowledge the work,
But never pierce the shell. But she sees me.

. . .

. . .

PENNY   [I do see you.]

. . .

. . .

RUTH *(to* CAL*)*   It was the most shocking thing.
Literally.

When she turned and looked at me that first time,
I dropped,
I was putting gas in my damn car,
And I dropped the hose. Right there.
Cost me two dollars in gas,
All over the concrete.
Puddles. Seeping through cracks. Draining my old life
away with it.
And I was empty. I was just, me.
Not the many things I'd put inside myself all those years—
The bits I'd stocked on the shelves of my rib cage—
Polite Smiles, Straight A report cards, Genteel Nodding,
Diplomas—
I was emptied out. I was purified. I longed to be filled,
by her.

PENNY   I was so angry.

RUTH   I didn't know that then.

PENNY   I was so, bursting.
The first time I saw you, I shot you a look—

RUTH   Electric.

ROSIE   I don't want to hear—

CAL   Hush for a minute.

PENNY   That look could have shot you down dead.
I wanted to shoot everyone down dead.
(to CAL)
I had raised six hives. Six. By myself. Got my own first
crop.
Then he comes out and he says,
"Your mother and I have decided."

And I say, "Six hives. Six full harvests. Best honey you ever
tasted."
He turns back to the house, motions Momma to stay
inside.
I say, "Try some, Daddy."
And I reach out to him with a full spoonful, golden
threads drip
Off the sides,
Reaching out to him,
So happy. He should be satisfied.
Gold I mined myself, over a year, no help.
"Go ahead," I say, "Taste it. See if it's not just as good as
yours. See if it's not better. Come on. You say I have to
raise my own, prove I can do it, I done it. It's here. You
too 'fraid to taste it, 'cause you know, you know, it just as
good as yours. Almost time to retire, old man. Retire and
hand it over. I told you, I could do it."
Then Momma comes back to the porch, a full-up garbage
bag in her hand, knotted at the top.
She holds on to that top knot and swings it once, twice,
three times. It sails over the grass, lands without a sound.
The knot has come lose. My clothes spill out.
Daddy opens his hand, tosses the truck keys at me.
The golden threads slide coyly off the side of the spoon,
dribble down on to the keys, until they are covered in
slickness. Later, when I go to start the truck, I have to
suck the honey off them so they'll fit right in the ignition.
When I pulled into that gas station, I was so angry, I
thought I could ignite the fuel you spilled, just by looking
at it.

RUTH   You did. You burned up everything I was.
And I am grateful.
. . .
(to ROSIE*)*
I'm sorry.

I am not better than you.
I am not, at all,
I, there's still some dust on my shelves,
Inside, some residue from my old life,
From when I was a What, rather than a Who.
And sometimes that old dust—

ROSIE   Sucks.

RUTH   Yes. Monumentally sucks.

CAL *moves toward bedroom door.*

CAL *(softly to* ROSIE*)*   Baby . . .

ROSIE   . . .

ROSIE *pops open a beer. Gives it to* RUTH.

ROSIE   On the house.

RUTH   Thank you.

ROSIE *goes over to* K.

K *settles on a surplus army cot in the corner.* ROSIE *wraps her in a blanket.*

ROSIE   Good night, my girl.

K *burrows down into the blanket.*

K   [I love you.]
Ggghhh.

ROSIE   I love you, too.

ROSIE *goes to* CAL, *takes his hand, they exit to the bedroom.*

RUTH *and* PENNY *finish their beers.*

RUTH   . . .

PENNY   . . .

RUTH   I'd forgotten—

PENNY   What?

RUTH   I'd forgotten that you were so angry when we
met.
That we,
That that look, wasn't really meant for me.
It was, about you.

PENNY   Sure, it was meant for you.
Sure it was.
I just didn't know it at the time.

RUTH   . . .

PENNY   Come on, Ruth.

RUTH *drains her beer.*

RUTH   "For whither thou goest, I will go; and where
thou lodgest, I will lodge: thy people shall be my people,
and thy God my God."

PENNY   Let's go to bed.

RUTH   But that's not the end of the story.
The end of the story is, Ruth doesn't get to stay with
Naomi.

Ruth is forced to marry Boaz,
Leave her one true love,
So that her son Obed can inherit so that David can inherit
and become King.

PENNY   It's still a beautiful story.

RUTH   But that is how Ruth ends.
Alone.

PENNY   You are not Ruth.
You are not, that Ruth.
You are this Ruth, our Ruth.
Come up to bed.

RUTH *does not move.*

PENNY   You are the Ruth that I picked up in a gas
station parking lot,
And we are not ashamed of that.
You are the Ruth that laughed so hard the first time we
kissed that you spit Slushee into my mouth.
You are the Ruth that memorized every book at the library
on bees and then forgot to put on gloves when you
opened the hive.
You are not lost.
You are not wrong.
You do not have to go back.
. . .
Come to bed with me.

PENNY *reaches out her hand to* RUTH.

K *begins to hum.*

RUTH *takes* PENNY*'s hand.*

K *(sings* Honeysuckle Rose*)*   Every honeybee fills with
jealousy when they see you out with me:
I don't blame them goodness knows, Honeysuckle Rose.

RUTH *and* PENNY *dance.*

K *(sings)*   When you're passin' by flowers droop and sigh,
And I know the reason why;
You're much sweeter goodness knows, Honeysuckle Rose.
Don't buy sugar, you just have to touch my cup.
You're my sugar; much sweeter when you stir it up.

RUTH *and* PENNY *swing; intimate laughter.*

They are closer to the ladder to the loft.

K *(sings)*   When I'm takin' sips from your tasty lips,
Seems the honey fairly drips;
You're confection goodness knows, Honeysuckle Rose.
Honeysuckle Rose.

RUTH *and* PENNY *kiss and climb the ladder, exit to the loft.*

K *is left alone.*

*Warm light streams through the cream and white paper that
covers the back wall of the barn: the transcendent connection
between* K*'s seen and unseen worlds.*

K *(looks at her empty hands)*   My doorknob.
A reminder of another world.
An escape hatch,
To Grandma's bedroom,
When they came to get me,
After she died. Her sunset glory.

When they came, I couldn't stuff my pockets with her
records,
Or her lace tablecloth or the picture of her son long dead
in Iraq.
I ran to her bedroom, slamming against each corner,
Something somewhere,
A rabbit hole.
A black hole.
Nothing.
Fuck you, Lewis Carroll and Dr. Who.
So when they dragged me out by my feet,
Screaming,
Like when I was born, to a new life,
A failed Apgar score,
When they dragged me out,
I grabbed the bedroom doorknob and they pulled me so
hard,
Popping my shoulder, leaving stretch marks on my waist,
That the crystal knob came off in my hand.
I shoved it into my pocket before they saw and asked and
wanted to sell it to pay the hospital bills.
. . .
Today,
When I fell out the boat.
Water breaking over me,
Heralding.
I reached for the doorknob in my pocket
To conjure her, her place, her smell, her time,
The safety of her,
And it was gone.
I reached further into the water, down beneath the sand
and the soil.
I forced my fingers down through roots of the cypress
trees and scared away the egrets.
I reached beneath the beneath,

Fit between grains of sand so small, they sang to one
another,
But it was gone.
That's when I tripped, in the seeking of it.

End of Act I

Act Two
1. Early the Next Morning

Daybreak light rolls in lazy.

K *on her cot, sleeps.*

CAL *enters. No shirt. Shaking off sleep. Checks on* K, *father-like, tucks in safe. Then reaches behind bar. Cracks a beer.*

ROSIE *(off-stage, sleepily)* [Come] Back to bed, baby.

CAL   Shhh. K's 'sleep.

Off-stage, in the distance, set back deep in CAL*'s memory, the sound of waves. Water kisses land, the echoing clang of buoy bells, the soft grind of gears through water. The waves.*

CAL *looks longingly out at the sea in his mind. Finishes his beer. Looks to his room with* ROSIE. *And then back out at the sea.*

K *stirs awake, she slides out of the blanket, goes to* CAL, *leans against him.*

CAL   You hear 'em too?
K *sleepily shakes her head "no."*

CAL   No.
'Course not.
It follows me.

A sharp clang.

CAL *(to* K*)* Early in the morning, the water shifts with
the new dawn,
For a few minutes, the sun's rays hit just right, and light
reflects off the pipes below the rig like a sea of stars.
A night sky under your feet.
And between the night sky below and the morning sky
above,
It's like you're sat at the first moment of creation with the
Maker Himself when there's only light. No land. No
water. None of us. Just peace.
(pointing to K*)*
The sea isn't haunted, little one. Not like the land. Not
like this place.

K   Ghhspppt . . .
(struggles to speak)
I I I I I . . .
(gives up, sings)
Nearer my God to Thee, Nearer to Thee.

CAL   Yeah, that's you, little K.
Nearer than Rosie and I, anyways.
You take good care of our Rosie when I'm gone.

K   Dddddghhht . . .
[Don't go.]

CAL   Shhh, shhh, now.

ROSIE *enters, dressed for the day, carries a coffee mug.*

CAL *(looks to* ROSIE*)* We just all pulled through life like
an invisible pipe to the sea, tryin' to avoid a blow out.

The sounds of the oil rig recedes.

CAL *(to* ROSIE *)*   Hey baby.

ROSIE *kisses him.*

ROSIE *(to* K*)*   Morning bathroom, love.

CAL *(to* K*)*   Come on, Miss K, up an' at 'em.

CAL *helps* K *to the bathroom on her injured ankle.*

RUTH *climbs down from the loft. She looks like hell warmed over.*

ROSIE *(re:* RUTH*)*   . . .
Shit.

RUTH   Don't say anything.
Please, just don't—

ROSIE *hands* RUTH *her coffee cup.*

RUTH   Thank you.

ROSIE   Got to give somebody His due,
Never thought I'd see you up before Penny.

RUTH   I haven't slept yet, not really.

ROSIE   Well, join the club.
Though, mine's pro'lly for better reasons than yours,
By the look of ya.

RUTH   It's good to have him home?

ROSIE   Always.

RUTH   I'm sorry to hear that he has to return so soon.
It doesn't seem fair that—

ROSIE   He volunteered for it.
He don't think I know, but . . .
The things we know are usually standing right next to the
things we don't. All we got to do is reach over and tap 'em
on the shoulder.

RUTH   Oh,
I'm . . . sorry?

ROSIE   It is what it is.

RUTH   Have you ever gone to therapy about it or—

ROSIE   Listen, I'm not sick in the head! We're not—

RUTH   Sorry, forget I asked.

ROSIE *takes* RUTH*'s coffee mug away, exits.*

RUTH *(calls to her off-stage)*   I really,
I've just got a talent for putting my foot in things here.
I never used to take a wrong step but now,
I feel like I'm dancing with two left feet to music I've
never heard.

ROSIE *returns with two mugs of coffee. Gives* RUTH *one.*

ROSIE   Don't talk. Just drink.

RUTH   . . .

ROSIE . . .

RUTH . . .

. . .

. . .

I was just thinking—

ROSIE *(as in "why are you talking")*   Oh my god,
seriously.

RUTH   It's me you don't like, really—

ROSIE   I really don't like either of you.
I don't hate you particularly but—

RUTH   For the most part, I've been the one making
trouble,
Out of step, with—

ROSIE   Seems like you always felt that way,
That's how you ended up here.

PENNY *(from off-stage loft)*   Hon?

ROSIE *[as in, "I am never gonna be allowed to finish my
coffee."]*   Oh, crackers.

RUTH *(calls up)*   Down here.

PENNY *comes down the ladder.*

ROSIE *swipes* RUTH*'s coffee cup again and takes the mugs into
the kitchen.*

PENNY *(to* RUTH*)*   I came up with a slogan.

RUTH   For your honey?

PENNY   For our honey.
I went to bed with you on my mind,
And this in the works
(holds up small glass jar of glistening honey)
I got up, tasted it, and just knew, it just came to me . . .
(envision this:)
New Sweet Potato Honey.
Two Southern favorites in one jar.
Get twice the Honeys for your honey today.

RUTH   . . .

PENNY   Get it?
(points to self)
Honey.
(points to RUTH*)*
Honey.
Twice the Honeys for your honey.

RUTH   Yes, wow, that's—

PENNY   You hate it.

RUTH   No! No. I just. I was thinking. Last night made
me—

PENNY   You haven't slept. Let's talk after you sleep.

ROSIE *re-enters.*

PENNY   Hey, Rosie!
(envision)
New Sweet Potato Honey.
Two Southern favorites in one jar.

Get twice the Honeys for your honey today.
Available online! Ships all over the country!
(to RUTH*)*
We'll make more money than Daddy ever did.
Drive right up to the door of his Church in a big BMW
one Sunday.
Roll down the window.
Look out at folks as they walk in, turnin' their heads,
whisper behind hands, "Who's that, who that be? Don't
she look like she's doin' good for herself."
And when Momma and Daddy come through, I'll make
sure they see, what I got. A big car, beautiful woman on
my arm, smilin' so wide, my happiness a sword and them
without a shield and I will wait 'til they get close and I
will lean out the window, and I will spit on them. I will
spit right on them. In front of everyone. In front of the
church. I will show them how good I am and how happy
I can be and how wrong they all were, because I'm sitting
there in that car, with this woman, smilin', in front of their
own church, and even God don't dare strike me down.

CAL *and* K *enter, sit. They're both dressed in new day clothes.*

ROSIE   Well, I don't have an internet connection and I
don't know about—

PENNY   The library does.
And we can sell it, here, too.
Come on out to the Palmetto Bar, come meet—

ROSIE   /Wait wait wait wait wait wait./

PENNY   /The Sweet Potato Honey ladies!/

PENNY *holds out the jar to* CAL *and* K.

PENNY *(to* CAL *and* K*)*   Go 'head and try it.

ROSIE   No no no no no no—

CAL *and* K *taste it. They exchange glances that mean, "It's good!"*

CAL   It can't hurt.

ROSIE *(to* CAL, *re: contradicting her)*   Oh, wow, was that a bad idea—

CAL   I like the idea of someone, someones, being here.
Just in case, when I'm gone.
If something were to happen—

ROSIE   Then stay.
Don't be gone.

CAL   I can't.

ROSIE   . . .

CAL   . . .

PENNY   We could.
We could stay. Harvest in the summer. Make jars. Market.
Send them out.
Just think, we could pay you double, triple what you're
asking for the loft.
And folks'll come here for the honey, stay for a drink or
two or six.

ROSIE   —or two or six—

PENNY   —and leave with some honey.

ROSIE   I don't like having you here.
You're not good for K.

RUTH   Opening the hives too far, that was my fault.

PENNY *(to* RUTH*)*   Stop apologizing.

RUTH   And the boat thing was an accident.
It coulda happened to anyone.

ROSIE   Her apology don't balance out the pain.

RUTH   Maybe I should go—

PENNY   Quit!

RUTH   Maybe this was, a fool's errand—

PENNY   Stop it now!

RUTH *(to* PENNY*)*   Maybe you should think about
coming up to live with me in Tallahassee.

ROSIE *(to* PENNY*)*   You should listen to your woman.

PENNY *(to* ROSIE*)*   You need us here.

ROSIE   It's not need. It's what havin' you here means.
It means that we're all right with what you do.
It means that we're throwing dirt in the face of your
family,
Who's been here as long as us, and never did us wrong.
It means puttin' ourselves out for you, in the community.
It means . . .

ROSIE *looks to* CAL.

ROSIE   It means,
When he's ready, he's still not gonna come back,
'Cause he thinks we don't need him.
'Cause there won't be any room.

CAL   [Not again. Not now.]
. . .

ROSIE *exits.*

CAL *gets another beer.*

RUTH *(to* PENNY*)*   Hon, maybe we should just go—

PENNY   This is my home! Mine, you get it,
You fuckin',
You run away every chance you get because you're weak.
Always apologizing an' I gotta stand up for you 'cause you
can't do it yourself.

RUTH   I'm sorry that you feel—

PENNY   There you go again!
Stop apologizing. Stop being sorry for your damn
existence.
I am not ashamed. I am who I am and this is my home
and they can all go fuck themselves if they think I'm ever
leaving. You are worthless to me. You run on back up
north. You run on back and put on your Halloween
costume of a life and publish your papers and write your
books and be nothing outside your picture on the cover.
You go on. I've had enough of you.

PENNY *charges the ladder and races up into the loft.
Disappears.*

RUTH   . . .

CAL   . . .

RUTH   . . .

CAL   . . .

K *finishes the honey.*

2. Later That Day

CAL*'s work gear and an oversized army surplus duffle bag are on the bar.*

ROSIE *sits at* K*'s table.* K *is not there.*

ROSIE *(calls off-stage to bedroom)*   Your socks are still damp.
They won't dry bunched up in your bag.
. . .
You need more talcum powder.
I have it on the grocery list for tomorrow morning.
If you could just wait—
(it sticks in her throat)
Get the truck looked at. The brakes sound close to dead.
An' K's out learnin' more 'bout those bees. She's gonna wanna show you, when she gets back.
An' you still need to look to—

CAL *enters with clothes, packs steadily.*

ROSIE   You don't have to be back 'til tomorrow night.

CAL   Someone should stop in the office. Before. And Tommy's not going to remember to do it. We'll be in the water, halfway out [to] the rig, and he'll realize he left the paperwork on dry ground. If we have to turn back, it'll eat up half a day.

ROSIE   Where'll you sleep?
You gotta sleep. You can't bed down in the office.

CAL   In the truck.

ROSIE   That's silly.
You got a clean bed here.
A bed with me in it.
And you got, I can make you, I gotta run out, but that
stew you like to take with you.
. . .

CAL   . . .
. . .

ROSIE   . . .
. . .
She loves you.

CAL   . . .
I don't know I deserve—

ROSIE   I love you.
She would like to have you home.
I would.

ROSIE *reaches out for him.*

CAL   Rosie!
It's your choice.
You pushed me out.

ROSIE   I never—

CAL   Once you took in . . . K.
And once you—

ROSIE   What I supposed to do?
That foster family woulda let her rot after the grandmother
died.

Woulda let her, lettin' her spend all day in the field, lookin'
up at the sun, burnt to a crisp, not eatin' right—

CAL   It wadn't as bad as—

ROSIE   You didn't see her!
An' what she ever asked of you anyways?

CAL   . . .

ROSIE   Huh?

CAL *throws gear into the bag with a clatter.*

ROSIE   Nothin'. Almost nothin'.
A little tuck in now an' 'gain.
To listen to a song.
To show you she ain't 'fraid of the bees no more, that she
can work 'em a li'l bit.
She just wants to love you, Cal, just let her. Let us.

CAL   . . .
It's not enough.

ROSIE   Not enough for—

CAL   Every day I walk through that door,
(looks to bedroom door)
I see failure.
(looks to K's table)

ROSIE *(this is news to ROSIE)*   Calvin.
You are not a failure.
No one would ever call you that.

CAL   I don't see that table.
I see your sister Kate laughing, too hard like always, so
hard, her mouth open and inviting, that I have to kiss her.

ROSIE   She's gone, Cal.
I hear up North somewhere.

CAL   I don't see that chair.
I see a picnic spread out on the beach. Your sister sneaking
a smoke and a soak in the sun with her bikini top flung off.
Over there, I see mother's disapproval.
There.
Your and Kate's father, shaking his head, sayin' it's a good
thing my father is dead because who'd wanna see this and
this is what happens when a boy ain't raised right and
what's wrong with me and he knows what's wrong and
you can't let the big head tell the little head what to do
and Jesus H. Fucking Christ, what the hell boy, I thought
you'd be a better man than this.

ROSIE *(low)*   Please stop.

CAL   And there.
Right there—
(K's cot)
I see a little ball of flesh, tucked down in the NICU.
And the nurses shaking their heads and looking to the
side,
Can't even look me in the eye,
Looking like, maybe it's best, maybe it's God's work,
This unimagined thing.
Unwanted children have it hardest of all.
Maybe God gonna take her home. Give her the good life
she'd never have down here.
And you're there, the only one not afraid to go right up to
her,

To gently stroke, whatever this thing is,
No matter where you stand—inside this place or out, in
this time or another—I always see you there.
Too young to be an Auntie.
Great big moon eyes.
Begging your sister and I to do somethin' different.
And you, closing those eyes,
Not speaking as we signed the papers to give her up.
As we said to the adoption lady, "No, just leave her name
K, leave it an initial, so her real family can give her the
name they want to call her."
Silent as you help your sister pack, and watched her away
from here.
Nothin' from you 'cept those big eyes for the baby who
weren't never supposed to be.
And she lived.
K lived.

ROSIE   She's tough. She got that from her Daddy.

CAL   Some days I wish she didn't.

ROSIE   You don't mean that.

CAL *(re: around him)*   It's all failure to me.
But out in the water.
Rig it, pull, water down the deck.
Tie up the big bear.
Keep an eye, don't let it blow out.
The CSG is too high, bring it round.
Tighten the drill string before you go on.
Out there, I'm free and righteous and strong. I am a man
that knows things, that does right, and has even saved a
few lives.
But here,
I did that to her.

Kate and I. Being stupid and too young and unprotected and,
She's paying, been paying, gonna keep paying.
There's nothing I can do about that.
It's a failure already found its end point.

ROSIE You match the water, you rip open the ocean floor, you bring up the blood of the earth. If you're strong enough for all that, then you're strong enough to face your child every day.
We can make her, as happy as she can be.
You're strong enough to sit still in one place for her, give up the waves to the ocean, and be happy sitting on the beach. Looking over creation and holding her little hand in yours.
That's what makes a man.

CAL *finishes packing.*

ROSIE . . .
. . .

CAL Not in the eyes of the world, Rosie.

ROSIE Aren't mine the only ones that count?

CAL *(kisses her)* No.
(deep sorrow, no meanness, just his own truth)
They don't count at all.

CAL *exits with bag.*

ROSIE . . .
. . .
. . .

ROSIE *notices he's left a shirt. She almost takes it to him, but then keeps it, breathes in his scent.*

ROSIE *refuses to cry. She cleans instead.*

ROSIE   . . .
. . .
. . .

K *and* RUTH *enter in basic bee keeper gear.*

K *walks over to* ROSIE, *she's so proud.*

K *hands* ROSIE *a jar of honey, motions for her to taste it.*

ROSIE *does. It's good.*

ROSIE   It's so good, K.

RUTH   She is turning into a great bee keeper.

ROSIE   All the hives make it in the move back?

RUTH   Yes.
Penny should be able to keep them outside as long as it's warm out.

ROSIE   Just Penny?

RUTH *(to* K*)*   How about you go upstairs and show Penny what you made? I'm sure she'll want to see it.

K *exits to the loft.*

RUTH   I think I should go.

ROSIE   She'll simmer down.

RUTH   Maybe but I, I don't, maybe this isn't who I am.

ROSIE   Oh, it's who you are.

RUTH   But maybe, I mean, let's look at this rationally.
I was tenured. I was researching and teaching.
But I was bored. I was feeling stifled,
Doing the same things,
Talking to the same people,
Mired in the same academic red tape,
Then I turned fifty and I start having panic attacks.
First at home, then in the lab, and then in class—
Which is the worst because the others, no one knows
about—
I'm encouraged to take time off. And then forced to.
Because I can't, walk into a classroom,
Talk about future evolutionary theory and how they're
going to pioneer the new world,
After I'm dead.
Dead. And alone. Alone until I am dead.
Because we live in a youth culture
And who wants a fifty-year-old bag of bones
Who isn't even brave enough to admit to herself that . . .
So I treat myself to a trip down the coast.
And I rent a car and I drive out to the beach.
And then to the casinos.
And then to a spa.
And then to another beach.
And then I buy the car because I've rented it so long, I
almost own it anyway.
And nothing feels right. No matter where I go . . .
I'm going broke trying to find me.
How fuckin' ridiculous is . . .
But then. Then.

On a dirt road off the interstate.
In a gas station parking lot,
I see her.
I see her angry and covered in sweat and righteous indig-
nation and kicking the absolute shit out of whatever is in
her way.
And a spike of heat shoots up my spine and I'm wetter
than I ever have been before.
And I finally admit to myself that I am,
That dreaded thing,
That mother always said not to be,
Because it will mean you will always be alone.
But I'm alone anyway.
And I'm fifty years old!
And I'm in a gas station parking lot.
And these things do not happen.

ROSIE   How much do you like fucking men?
And all that comes with it.

RUTH   . . . It's better than being hit by a truck.

ROSIE   A swarm of flies come straight outta your mouth
sometime.

RUTH   I know, I know.
Things come out of my mouth and it's meaningless.
It's just flies.

ROSIE   Yeah, it is.
And they say,
You take those flies,
Put 'em in a bottle,
Name 'em,
Throw 'em out into the Gulf.
They float away. All the lies and bullshit,

Float out into the ocean.
Get swept up, dispersed by the waves, 'til there's nothin'.
You're clean and good.
You can start again.

RUTH   Well, let's say I did.
Let's say, at fifty, after years of repression . . . this is me.
I still don't think that I love her.
Not in an Ever After way.

K *climbs down from the loft.*

ROSIE   There you are, my girl.

ROSIE *tries to be cheery.*

ROSIE   How's Penny like that honey? She said you did
good, right? You did so good.

K   . . .

ROSIE   You wanna sing, baby.
Go ahead.
We could use a lift.

ROSIE *returns to cleaning.*

K *(sings* Mood Indigo*)*   You ain't been blue,
No no, no, no.
You ain't been blue,
'Til you've had that mood indigo.

PENNY *appears on the top of the loft.*

K *(sings)*   That feeling goes stealin',
Down to my shoes,

While I sit and sigh;
"Go 'long blues."
Always get that mood indigo, since my baby said goodbye.
In the evenin' when lights are low,
I'm so lonesome I could cry.
'Cause there's nobody who cares about me,
I'm just a soul who's bluer than blue can be,

PENNY*'s on the ladder.*

K *and* PENNY *finish the song together.*

K / PENNY *(sings)*   When I get that mood indigo,
I could lay me down and die.

PENNY   . . .
. . .

RUTH   . . .
. . .

ROSIE   That's beautiful, K.

K *embraces* ROSIE *as hard as she can.*

As PENNY *and* RUTH *continue their silent exchange, who is
going to talk first, and just what the hell do you say?*

ROSIE *separates slightly from* K:

ROSIE *(to* K*)*   What's wrong, girl?

K   . . .

ROSIE   Come on, now.
It can't be as bad as all that.

K *picks up* CAL*'s shirt that he's accidentally left behind. The same one* ROSIE *held earlier.*

K *(sings low and rough)*   Always get that mood indigo,
since my baby said goodbye.
In the evenin' when lights are low,
I'm so lonesome I could cry.

ROSIE   Oh, honey, it's not your fault.
He just, can't, is all.
Come on, let's get you some lunch.

ROSIE *and* K *exit.*

PENNY *and* RUTH *are left alone.*

PENNY   /I probably should/

RUTH   /I probably should/

They gesture to each other: no, you go first; no, you can go first.

PENNY   /Apologize./

RUTH   /Apologize./

PENNY   This isn't what I thought it would be.

RUTH   I tried to not think about what I thought it would be.
So you're ahead of me, is the point.

PENNY   I'm sorry that I said,
I'm not really sick of you.

RUTH   But you are. I'm sick of me.

PENNY   Baby, we'll just,
Just let's get through this season.
We'll set up the website and harvest the—

RUTH   I cannot thank you enough for,
Being that mirror,
That fearless,
That truth that,
For all intents and purposes—

PENNY   For all intents and purposes, what?
Just stay the night.

RUTH   No, this isn't my life. This isn't my—

PENNY   But it is your life. You are—

RUTH   This is myself.
And I will always thank you for giving it to me.
But it's not my life.
I've got to go put myself back in my life and make it work.
I would never work here.

PENNY   . . .
Are you sure?

RUTH   No, but . . .

PENNY *embraces* RUTH.

PENNY   You are the best middle-age pussy I ever had.

RUTH *laughs.*

The light fades on the women.

They rest in stillness.

*Transcendent light streams through the paper on the back
wall of the barn.*

K   After they drank, Ruth left.
Penny and Rosie went to bed.
I picked up Rosie's bottle and walked all night.
Down the gravel road,
Along the field where Rosie found me,
To the interstate,
Around to exit 4 to the beach,
Along the edge of the sand to the oil office.
Cal's truck parked outside.
The field of new poured asphalt seemed to shift under me
As I made my way to the truck and knocked on the
window.
He jumped when he saw me.
Got out.

CAL *appears.*

K   Says,

CAL   What you doin' here girl?

K   And,

CAL   You should be home in bed.

K   He took me into the office to call Rosie but I cut off
the phone before he could dial.
I handed him the bottle.
I caught a fly.

I took a piece of paper and I wrote "K" on it.
But when I tried to put it in the bottle with the fly,
He stopped me.

CAL   No, not K. I'm not throwin' you out.

K   He told me to wait there,
And he turned away.
And he wrote a list of things, that I couldn't see but,
It was a really long list.
When he was done, he looked it over, rolled it up, and put
his sins in the bottle with the fly.
Then we walked down to the beach; it was almost dawn.
And he told me how my mother walked here,
Sunbathed here
Laughed here.
Cried here after I was born.
Then when the story was done,
He took the bottle, and threw it into the ocean, past the
break,
So the waves carried it away.
And we walked home hand-in-hand.

CAL *and* K *take each other's hand.*

K *(sings* Come Rain or Come Shine*)*   I'm gonna love you
like nobody's loved you, come rain or come shine.
High as a mountain and deep as a river, come rain or come
shine.
I guess when you met me it was just one of those things,
But don't ever bet me 'cause I'm gonna be true if you let
me love you.
You're gonna love me like nobody's loved me, come rain
or come shine.
Happy together, unhappy together, and won't it be fine.

Days may be cloudy or sunny. We're in or we're out of the money,
But I'm with you always, I'm with you rain or shine.

Lights fade.

End of Play

Music

The song rights for public performance (live, acapella, no recording) are held by Warner/Chappell Music Inc. as of March 2017 for these four songs:

"Honeysuckle Rose" (1929) by Andy Razaf and Thomas Waller
https://www.ascap.com/repertory#ace/search/workID/380068275

"Dream a Little Dream of Me" (1931) by Gus Kahn, Wilbur Schwandt, and Fabian Andree
https://www.ascap.com/repertory#ace/search/workID/340075832

"In the Still of the Night" (1937) by Cole Porter
https://www.ascap.com/repertory#ace/search/workID/390130339

"Come Rain or Come Shine" (1946) by John Mercer and Harold Arlen
https://www.ascap.com/repertory#ace/search/workID/330077840

Contact: (310) 441-8600, Jeremy.blietz@warnerchappell.com
c/o WB Music Corp, Warner Chappell Music, 10585 Santa Monica Blvd, Los Angeles, California 90025

The song rights for public performance (live, acapella, no recording) are held by Sony ATV as of March 2017 for this song:

"Mood Indigo" (1931) by Edward Kennedy Ellington, Irving Mills, and Barney Bigard
https://www.ascap.com/repertory#ace/search/workID/430083804

Contact: (615) 726-8300, livestageinquiries@sonyatv.com
424 Church Street, Suite 1200, Nashville, Tennessee 37209

A list of replacement public domain songs is available from the playwright.